FUN

MW00977737

Lonely Girl

No Time to Scream

Anna Higgins

Anna Higgins

All illustrations by George Craig

Cover design: John Grain

Copyright © 2013 Anna & Sydney Higgins

All rights reserved.

ISBN-10: 1482325152
ISBN-13: 978-1482325157

TWO

FUN READ

STORIES

LONELY GIRL

by

ANNA HIGGINS

1

Judy was out of breath.

There was a pain in her side

but she kept on running.

Tina West and her gang

were after her.

They had chased her

all the way from school

and they were catching up.

Judy ran around

a group of kids

playing in the street.

One of the boys tried to stop her.

She pushed him over

and ran on.

The boy got up.

He shouted at Judy

and ran after her.

His mates followed.

Now there was

a crowd of boys and girls,

all trying to catch Judy.

She was tall,

had long legs

and could run quickly.

But she didn't feel

she could run much further –

and the crowd was catching up.

Judy lived two streets away,

past the club where her father

often went to drink

and past some houses

that were being pulled down.

She knew she would be caught

before she got home.

Then she had an idea.

There was a little shop

round the next corner.

She would run in there.

It was owned by Mr and Mrs Lamb,

a kind old pair,

who had lived there

for over thirty years.

Now the houses in the street

were being pulled down,

Mr and Mrs Lamb weren't very busy.

The people in the new flats

didn't use their shop

but went to the supermarket

to do their shopping.

When Judy ran into the shop,

Mr Lamb was eating some crisps.

He asked Judy what she wanted.

Judy fought to get her breath.

'They're chasing me,' she gasped,

'Tina West and her mates.'

Mr Lamb ate another crisp.

'Look!' said Judy,

still out of breath.

'They're waiting outside.'

Mr Lamb looked at the kids

and then went to the door.

'Clear off! Hop it!'

he shouted at them,

waving his arms.

He waited until all the kids

had gone off down the street.

Then he went back into the shop.

'Well, young lady,' he said,

'you'd better tell me

what this is all about.'

'We had a row at school,' she said,

'and Tina said she was going

to beat me up.'

'I don't know, I'm sure,'
said Mr Lamb, shaking his head.
'Girls these days seem
just as bad as the boys.
Now when I was a young …'

'They've all gone now,' Judy said.
'I'd better get back home now.
Thanks for what you did.'

Judy ran as fast as she could.
She went the back way,
just in case anyone was waiting
round the corner.
She ran down an alley by the club
and on through a back yard
where she climbed over a wall.
Then she was home.

She pushed open the back door

and went into the kitchen.

As usual, it was in a mess.

Unwashed cups and plates

were piled by the sink.

Food left over from lunch

was still on the table.

Dirty clothes had been thrown

on the floor and the back of chairs.

The house was far too small

for so many people.

There were only four rooms –

two bedrooms upstairs

and the kitchen and lounge downstairs.

There wasn't any garden,

only a small backyard,

and the front door opened

right onto the street.

Judy lived in the house

with her mum and dad,

her three brothers

and her grandma.

Judy had to share

one of the two bedrooms

with her grandma.

The boys had the other one,

while her mum and dad

slept on a sofa-bed

in the front room.

It was gran's house really.

They had all gone to live there

a long time ago,

when her dad lost his job.

Her mum liked to be with gran

and she liked having a gossip

with the women living in the street.

Her dad liked in there too.

It was close to the club

where he spent lots of time

with all his mates.

He said he didn't want to live in a flat.

'I'd break my neck

falling down the stairs

one night when I came home drunk,'

he often told Judy.

Judy's three brothers liked it there.

They played with all the other kids

who lived in the street.

It was only Judy who hated it.

There was nowhere in the house

where she could be alone.

But she hated school even more.

That day had been the worst ever.

Her bag had been stolen

and her things thrown

all over the playing field.

When Judy found out

what had been done,

she was very upset.

She sat down and cried.

Then a girl told her

that Tina and her friends

had taken the bag.

Judy looked at them

and saw they were laughing,

For a second, she was so angry

she couldn't move.

Then she stood up

and waved her fists at them.

She was so angry

that she raced towards the girls.

Tina didn't have time to move

before Judy jumped on her,

kicking and screaming.

Judy bit and scratched.

A crowd gathered round

as Tina tried to fight back.

Then Tina's friends managed

to pull Judy away,

leaving Tina scratched and cut.

That was why, after school,

Tina and her gang had chased Judy.

For once, Judy was glad to be home.

She crept quietly upstairs.

Her dress was torn and dirty.

So she took it off and stood

looking at herself

in her gran's mirror.

Judy didn't like her body.

Her breasts were very small –

they didn't even fill her bra –

and her long legs were like sticks.

She shrugged, turned away

and put on a clean dress.

2

Judy was a strange girl,

not a bit like the other girls at school.

She liked to be quiet and

she liked to be on her own.

Much of the time, she didn't listen

to what other people were saying.

She was always dreaming.

This got her into a lot

of trouble at school

and meant that

she didn't have many friends.

She wasn't keen on the same things

as all the other girls.

She didn't like pop music.

She didn't like dancing.

She didn't have a mobile phone.

She didn't have a boyfriend.

Although she had long legs

and could run quickly,

she wasn't good at games.

When she played hockey

or football, or tennis,

she was often dreaming.

Then she would miss the ball

and the rest of the team

would shout at her.

Last term, some of the girls

had started making fun of Judy

because, even though she was nearly fifteen,

her periods had not begun.

Her mum told her

it was nothing to worry about

but she did take her to see the doctor.

He told her it was quite normal.

Sure enough, her first period

came in the Easter holidays

but, even after that,

girls at school still teased her.

This upset Judy.

She'd find a place to hide

and then have a good cry.

The teachers were no help.

They seemed to think

that Judy was a problem pupil.

After the fight with Tina,

life at school was even worse.

During every break,

Tina and her gang of friends

would search for Judy.

When they found her,

they would tease and torment her.

There were some girls in Judy's class

who didn't like what was going on

but, if they said anything,

Tina and her mates

went for them as well.

So nobody was nice to Judy.

She had no friends.

Nobody dared speak to her.

Judy was alone.

It was a large school

with lots of pupils.

When the bell went for break,

all the teachers rushed

to their staff-room

and stayed there until break was over.

None of them was aware

of what was going on.

Judy had never hurt anyone.

She couldn't understand

why the girls were so nasty to her.

At first, she tried to pretend

she didn't care.

After a few weeks,

Judy couldn't bear it any more.

She begged Tina to leave her alone

but Tina just laughed.

The next day, Judy pretended

that she was ill.

Her mum let her stay home

but, after two days, she said that

Judy had to go back to school.

Judy couldn't face it.

Instead of going to school,

she spent the day

walking around the shops.

By the time school ended,

she was sick with hunger –

she'd had no money for food.

But she didn't mind.

It was so much better

than being at school.

On Monday, her mother gave her

the week's dinner money

and so, instead of going to school,

she was went to a small café.

She was sitting drinking a coffee

when a young lad with long hair

walked up to her table.

'You out of work too?' he asked.

Judy looked up in surprise.

'No! Well … yes, I suppose so,'

she said.

'Got any money?' he asked.

Judy shook her head.

'How about the cinema?

I know a back way in,'

he said quietly,

'and so it won't cost anything.'

Judy didn't think twice.

She was bored and fed up.

So she said she'd go.

'I'm Dave,' said the lad

as they left the café.

Judy followed him.

They went down a side street,

through a car park and,

after climbing over a wall,

they arrived

at the back of a cinema.

Dave pointed

to a small, open window,

high up in the wall.

'I'll push you up through there,'

he told her. 'Then you come back

and open that side door

so I can get in.'

Judy looked up in horror

at the small window.

'Get lost!' she said.

'I'm not going through that.

You'll have to do it.'

'I can't. It's the Ladies toilet,'

he hissed. 'Come on.

I'll buy you an ice-cream inside.'

'Stuff your ice-cream,'

Judy said sharply.

'Oh, well, if you're that feeble!'

said Dave and turned to go.

Judy couldn't bear

to see him go away.

She had no other friend.

'O.K. I'll try,' she said.

Dave bent down
and cupped his hands
to give Judy a lift up.

She grabbed at the window ledge
and tried to pull herself up.
After a lot of effort,
she was able to clamber
through the open window.
Inside, she fell to the floor.

'Now I've caught you,'
said a sharp voice.

To Judy's horror, she saw
a large women with arms folded
standing in the doorway of the Ladies.
She had a nasty look in her eyes
and a half-smile on her face.

She went to grab Judy

and shouted,

'I'm taking you to the manager.'

Judy jumped up.

'Run!' she shouted to Dave

through the open window.

It was too late.

Outside, there was a man

holding Dave

by the back of his jacket.

The woman grabbed Judy by the arm

and marched her through

the almost empty cinema

to the manager's office.

The manager was a little man

with small hard eyes,

a beak-like nose

and a bald head.

'I've called the police,'

he said in an icy voice.

Judy's body froze in terror.

Then David was dragged in.

He said nothing.

He just stared at the floor,

his face ugly with hate and anger.

The manager sat,

tapping his fingers on the desk.

He glared at Judy and Dave.

She wanted to scream

or faint or do anything

just so the waiting

would come to an end.

There was a knock on the door

and a policeman walked in,

leaving the door open.

Dave was standing near it

and suddenly he turned and ran.

Judy could hear him,

leaping down the stone stairs

that led to the plush carpets

in the cinema's entrance.

There was a lot of shouting

as the policeman and the manager

raced out after him.

Judy was left alone

with the woman who'd caught her.

She felt weak at the knees

and slumped down into a chair.

The two men came back without Dave

and began asking Judy questions.

The policeman could see

she was telling the truth.

He told the manager

to give her a warning

and then he said

he would take Judy home

to let her parents know

what she'd been up to.

Judy began to cry and begged him

not to tell her parents.

'You should think yourself lucky!'

said the manager angrily.

'I'm fed up with you kids

sneaking in here,

tearing the place up

and causing trouble.'

Judy said nothing.

'If I ever catch you
doing it again,' the manager said.
'I'll make sure
you end up in court.'

Judy said she was sorry
and then the policeman
took her out to his car.
She sat in the back,
silent and shaking.
The policeman told her that
Dave had got away.
Judy was glad.

The police car stopped
outside her house.

Without even looking,

Judy knew that,

all down the street,

curtains were being pulled open

and all the nosey people

were gawping at her.

3

Judy's parents were very upset.

Her mum kept on

about how everybody in the street

must have seen the police

bringing Judy back home.

Her dad lost his temper

and hit her with his belt.

It didn't seem to matter

what she did or said,

everyone was against her.

Alone in the bedroom,

she sobbed and sobbed.

In time, she cried herself to sleep.

Her gran woke her up

when she came up to bed.

Judy lay still and quiet.

Inside, she felt cold and hard.

Nobody wanted her.

Nobody cared how she felt.

She thought of Dave

and how his face had looked

after he'd been caught.

Now she knew that he had

the same hatred as she did.

She'd run away to find him.

Judy waited till gran

began to snore.

Then she crept downstairs.

The house was still and quiet.

She opened her mum's bag

and took out all the money.

Then she put on her coat

and crept out the back door.

Judy had no idea of where to go.

She didn't even know Dave's full name

or where he lived.

She spent the night

walking around the town,

hiding every time a car went by.

By morning, she was cold,

worn out and hungry.

She went to the café

where she had met Dave,

hoping he would turn up.

She sat there for hours.

After a time,

her eyelids began to close

and she fell asleep.

She was woken up

by a woman shaking her.

'You can't sleep here,'

she was saying.

Judy stood up

and walked out in a daze.

Near to the café was the Town Hall,

a large place with lots of steps

leading up to the entrance.

Judy stumbled across to them

and sat down,

her head in her hands.

She just wanted to cry.

Judy hadn't noticed that,

a little further away,

a lad was sitting on the steps,

hunched into his coat.

After a while, he got up

and walked up to her.

Judy didn't move.

Then he said to her,

'Sorry about yesterday.'

Judy looked up, dazed.

It was Dave.

She looked at him and smiled.

'I've found you,' she said.

'You're not going

to turn me in?' he said.

Judy laughed.

'I've run away to find you,'

she told him.

'I've got some money –

not much, but something.

Where can we go?'

At first, Dave wasn't keen

but, as he had no money

and nothing else to do,

he said he'd go along.

They decided to get

out of town.

First they bought

some bread and cheese

and then two bottles of beer.

Next, they caught a bus

to Hopton, a village

out in the country.

Sitting with Dave

as the bus drove slowly

along country lanes,

Judy felt happier

than she had ever been.

They both went to sleep on the bus

and they had to be woken up

when they got to Hopton.

They watched the bus turn round

and go back to the town.

Not knowing what to do next,

they set off walking

down a muddy farm track.

They sat under a tree

and ate their bread and cheese.

But it was getting late.

Judy began to wonder

what her parents were doing.

Just as it was getting dark,

they came to an old cottage

that had been empty for years.

There were holes in the roof

and the branches of a tree

were growing though a hole

in one of the stone walls.

Most of the windows were broken

and the front door

was hanging off its hinges.

Dave kicked it open.

'We can sleep here, Judy,'

said Dave, taking her by the hand.

Judy wasn't too keen

but she was getting a little scared

of being outside as it got darker.

They pushed their way inside.

It was damp and musty

and very creepy.

They cleared a space on the floor

and sat down on Dave's coat.

It was very cold.

The wind began to blow

and the cottage creaked.

Judy held tight to Dave

and he tried to kiss her

but she was having none of it.

She was too scared.

Around them, inside the room,

there were many strange noises.

Something ran over Judy's leg

and she screamed.

Dave pointed to a cupboard

standing in the corner.

'Let's get in there,'

Dave said.

They squeezed into it

and hung onto each other,

terrified and very cold.

But the noises didn't stop.

The whole house seemed alive.

They couldn't stand it any longer.

They rushed out of the cupboard

and ran outside.

They kept on running

till the cottage was far behind.

It was daylight

when they got back to town.

Dave and Judy said goodbye

at the end of her road.

Judy was too tired to care

about the trouble

that awaited her.

She felt she could face anything

as long as she was safe at home.

She did get into trouble

but her mum and dad

were so glad to have her back,

safe and sound,

that they didn't make too much fuss.

When Judy went back to school,

all the girls seemed to know

that she'd run away from home.

They asked many questions

but Judy told them very little.

After a few weeks,

the girls at school

left her alone

but they no longer teased her.

Still without any friends,

Judy tried her best

to try and forget

all that happened.

NO TIME TO SCREAM

by

ANNA HIGGINS

When Sally returned home from school

and opened the front door,

her two baby brothers

were still crying.

'Is that you, Sal?'

her mother called.

'Yes, mum,' shouted Sally,

as she took off her coat.

'Give us a hand, will you?

The twins won't eat their tea.'

In the kitchen, two fat babies

were sitting in two high chairs.

Their faces were red with anger

and their podgy fists

were pushing away the food

they were being given.

'They've been like this all day,'

Sally's mum said wearily.

'I don't know what's wrong.'

'Little brats!' Sally said angrily

as she took the food from her mum.

Sally's mum was in a state.

Her hair was uncombed

and her apron was stained and dirty.

The kitchen was just as bad.

There were toys on the floor,

dirty washing in a corner,

half-eaten food on the table

and potato peelings in the sink.

Sally hated it all.

She hated the mess

and the noise that never stopped.

She felt sorry for her mother.

There were five children

in the family.

Sally was the eldest.

She was fourteen and she had

a sister of eleven

and a brother of nine.

The twins, both boys,

were only nine months old.

Sally's dad told her

they were 'a slip up'.

They were too much for her mum

and so Sally tried to help.

So did her dad

but he was a bus driver

and he wasn't home much

because he did a lot of overtime

to earn enough money

to feed everybody.

Sally got the twins

to eat their tea.

They'd made a lot of mess.

There was food in their hair,

on their hands

and all over their clothes.

The twins had to be washed

and have their clothes changed.

This made them cry again.

But when they were put into their cots,

they quickly went to sleep.

Sally made a cup of tea

and had something to eat.

'Where are the others?'

Sally asked her mum.

'I don't know,' her mum said.

'They're not back from school.

Go and see what they're up to.

There's a good girl.'

'All right,' said Sally.

'But them I'm going to Janet's

for a little while.

Sally was glad to get away

from the mess and the noise.

She hadn't gone far

when she saw a crowd of kids.

There was a fight going on.

Sally pushed through the crowd.

Her sister Anne was there –

and she was crying.

Sally soon saw why.

Peter, her brother,

was on the floor

and a much older boy

was sitting on him.

Pete was trying to get away

but the other boy

was punching him hard.

Sally got very angry.

She pulled the boy off

by his hair.

The boy shouted

and tried to hit Sally

but she pushed him hard

and he fell over.

'Clear off!' Sally shouted.

'And if you touch my brother again,

I'll kill you!'

The boy got up.

'You just watch it,' he said.

'I'll get my brother

to sort you out.

He'll jump on you

and he'll hit you

till your eyes pop out.'

Sally laughed

and the boy ran off.

Sally saw her brother and sister

safely back home

and then went to see Janet,

her best friend.

She lived just round the corner.

Janet had bought a CD

that Sally wanted to hear.

Sally had a great time at Janet's.

She liked being there.

Janet had a bedroom of her own

where they played music

and talked and laughed.

It had gone ten when Sally left.

As she was walking home,

she almost bumped into two lads

and one of them was

the boy who'd been fighting

her brother, Pete.

Sally turned and ran.

The boys shouted and chased after her.

Sally had no chance.

The big lad soon caught her

and grabbed her arm.

Sally was scared.

She could see the lad was grinning

and was enjoying himself.

'What's the rush then?'

the lad asked.

'Let go of me,' Sally cried.

'You're a big bully.'

'Now my kid brother tells me

you tried to pull all his hair out

and I don't allow that,'

he said with a laugh

as he slowly twisted

Sally's arm behind her back.

The younger boy ran up.

'Go on then, Mike,' he shouted.

'Smash her face in.'

'Can't do that,' laughed Mike.

'It would spoil her good looks.'

With that, he let Sally go

and she ran off home.

She was shaking and very upset

but she didn't say anything

to her mum and dad.

The next day, when she and Janet

were walking home from school,

a motorbike roared past them

and then stopped sharply.

As they walked towards it,

Sally saw that the rider was Mike,

the lad who had chased her

the night before.

'Come on! Run!' Sally shouted.

The two girls ran down the road.

The place was crowded.

There were women with prams

and little kids on bikes.

Sally and Janet ran round them

as best they could

but soon Mike on his motorbike

was riding beside them.

'Do you want a lift?'

Mike called to Sally.

She was a bit put out.

She had thought he was going

to be nasty to her again.

'No, I don't,' she shouted back.
'I wouldn't go anywhere with you.
You're a rotten big bully
and so is your brother!'

Janet couldn't work out
why Sally was so upset.
Mike looked pretty cool to her
and she'd have gone on his bike.
But Sally marched off
and Janet went after her.
Mike sat grinning on his bike.

The next day,
when Sally and Janet left school,
Mike was standing at the corner,
leaning against his motorbike.

Sally was going to walk by
but he stopped her.
'Look, pretty one,' he said softly.
'I'm sorry about the other night.'

At first,
Sally didn't know what to say.
Janet began to giggle.

'My name's not Pretty One,'
she said. 'It's Sally.'

'Right, pretty Sally,' Mike said.
'I'll take you home.'

Sally just stood there.

Then Janet gave her a push.
'Go on, Sally,' she said.
'See what it's like.'

'I've got a helmet for you,' Mike said.

Sally put on the helmet and then

got on the bike behind Mike.

The engine roared and they were off.

Sally hung on.

They seemed to be going very fast.

Mike passed cars and buses.

Shops and house flashed by.

The wind stung her face

and hurt her eyes.

She didn't know

where they were going.

Soon they were our of the town

on a long straight road.

They went faster and faster.

It seemed as though

they would take off

and fly through the air.

At last, Mike slowed down

and pulled off the road.

When Sally got off the bike,

she was shaking so much

she could hardly undo her helmet.

Mike grinned.

'How about that then, Sal?' he asked.

Sally wanted to say

that she hated it,

that she'd been scared stiff

and she wanted to go home

but she didn't want him

to laugh at her.

Anyway, she was still shaking

too much to speak and so

she sank down on the grass

and said, 'Great! Just great!'

'I knew you'd like it,' said Mike,

sitting down next to her.

'We were really burning it up.

Most birds would've been scared.'

'I don't scare easy,'

said Sally but she wished

she was safely at home.

Sally and Mike sat talking

for a long time.

Sally found out a lot about Mike.

He was seventeen

and was out of work.

The factory he'd gone to

after leaving school

had just closed down.

He was trying to get another job

so he could keep up

the payments on his bike.

'He's rather dishy,' Sally thought

as they sat talking.

'Not half as bad as he seemed.'

'Do you fancy coming to a disco

on Saturday?' Mike asked her.

Sally sat up.

'I'd love to,' she said.

She felt very happy.

'It's a date then,' he said

as he stood up.

'I'll pick you up at eight.'

As they rode back to town,

Sally held on tightly to Mike.

It was past seven

when they got back to Sally's house.

Her dad was standing outside.

He was very angry.

'Get inside,' he snapped at Sally.

'And you keep away from our Sal,'

he shouted angrily to Mike.

Her dad stormed into the house

and banged the door.

'I won't have you hanging around

with any Hell's Angels,'

he shouted at Sally

as she ran upstairs.

Sally was crying on her bed

when her mum came into the room.

Sally told her mum about Mike

and where they had been,

but she left out the bit

about doing a ton on the bike.

'He's not a Hell's Angel.

I like him,' Sally told her.

'And he's asked me to go with him

to a disco on Saturday night

but now I won't be able to go.'

Sally started to cry again.

'Don't cry, Sal,' her mum said.

'I'll speak to your dad.

He was worried about you.

That's why he was angry!'

Sally stopped crying

and they both went downstairs.

She tried to talk to her dad
but he was still angry.

'I'm not having you going about
with lads on motor-bikes,'
he told her firmly.
'They're up to no good
and you're having nothing
to do with them.
I know what they're like!'

The next day when Sally saw Mike,
she told him she couldn't go
to the disco on Saturday.

Mike laughed and said,
'Your old man goes out drinking
every Saturday night.
I'll get you home

long before he gets back.'

Sally agreed to go
but she was scared,
knowing her dad would go mad
if he found out.

On Saturday, Sally waited
until her dad went out
before she got ready.
She put on a new dress
her mum had bought her
a few weeks before.
Janet had lent her some new shoes
to wear with it.
That morning, she had bought
some false eyelashes
and she spent half an hour
trying to put them on.

It wasn't easy and she made

her eyes read and sore

but, when she'd finished

putting on her make-up,

she looked at herself in the mirror

and was very pleased with the result.

She looked older

and felt prettier.

She went downstairs

and peeped round the door.

Her mum was bathing the twins.

'I'm off to Janet's.' she said.

'See you later,' her mum called.

Sally had told Mike she'd meet him

outside the disco.

He was waiting for her there.

'You look great, Sally,'

he told her

as they went in.

Sally felt really grown up.

Everything was going well.

As the door opened,

she felt a blast of hot air

and heard loud music.

It was very dark inside

and crowded with dancers.

Sally loved dancing.

Music made her feel carefree.

She and Janet often danced

in Janet's bedroom

when she was playing

music that they liked.

Mike was a good dancer

and they moved well together.

Sally had never had such a good time.

After nearly an hour,

they had to sit down –

both of them were so hot.

Mike bought himself a beer

and Sally a soft drink.

She was happy to sit down

and watch the other girls

to see what they were wearing.

She saw lots of older girls there

from her own school.

One or two of them

spoke to her

and glanced at Mike.

Sally felt very happy.

After their drink, Mike took her

to meet some of his friends.

Sally forgot about the time.

When she did think about it,

it was too late.

Sally was very upset

when she saw that it was midnight.

She thought about her dad

and what he would do.

Mike was very sorry for he knew

that Sally would really get told off.

He and Sally rushed out.

The motorbike was round the corner.

Sally was crying.

She was afraid to go home.

Mike set off at great speed.

It was raining.

There was a lot of traffic

on the slippery roads.

Sally was too afraid of what

her dad was going to say

to worry about being on the bike.

She tried to work out

what she could say to her dad.

If she got off the motorbike

at the end of her road,

she could say she'd been at Janet's

but that was no good.

Her dad would have been there

already to fetch her,

If Mike took her home,

her dad would be waiting outside.

Mike was going fast.

He swung round a corner.

Sally felt the bike lean over

and then saw a bus

coming towards them.

Mike braked sharply,

the front wheel locked

and the bike began to skid.

Mike fought to keep control

but the bike shot sideways

across the wet road.

As they hit the pavement,

Mike was thrown clear

but Sally went with the bike

and ended up trapped beneath it.

It all happened so quickly that

Sally had no time to scream.

She just knew total panic

as she felt the bike go

and saw sparks fly

as metal scraped on the road.

Then the shiny wet pavement

rushed to hit her

and the world went blank.

Mike had known they were going

to crash as soon as the bike

began to skid.

In a panic, he had tried

to pull the bike out of the skid.

When they crashed

and he was thrown clear,

everything went deathly quiet.

In the silence

as he was shot from the bike,

he felt as though he was

a bundle of old rags

being thrown into the air.

He seemed to land

in piles of cotton wool,

falling softly down and down,

his arms and legs

folding gently under him.

The bus stopped.

People came out of their houses

and a crowd had soon gathered.

The back wheel of the motorbike

was trapping Sally's legs.
Her head had smashed
against the road.
Her helmet was still on
but it was badly dented,
Her arms were bent under her
and her face was grey.
She didn't move.
In the road was a pool of blood.

Mike lay some way off.
His helmet was split open.
He looked like a crushed leaf,
Blood was seeping out
from some cuts on his face
and trickling from his mouth
where some front teeth
had been knocked out.

A woman saw them and screamed.

Someone called an ambulance.

Two men lifted the bike off Sally

but nobody dared move her

until the ambulance arrived.

Mike was carried

to the side of the road.

It had just gone eleven o'clock

when Sally's dad arrived home.

Sally's mum was asleep

on the sofa but she woke up

and he asked her,

'Where's our Sal?'

'She's not home yet,' she said sleepily.

'What do you mean?' he shouted.

'I told her not to go out.

Where's she been? I'll flay her

if she's been out with that idiot!'

'Keep your hair on,' Sally's mum said.

'She's round at Janet's.'

'At this time of night!'

he shouted. 'Don't give me that!

I'll find out where she is.'

He rang Janet's mother

but she told him

she hadn't seen Sally all day.

He then phoned everybody

who might know where Sally was

but nobody knew anything.

Then he rang the police

but he was told

they knew nothing about Sally.

An ambulance had taken

Sally and Mike to the hospital.

Mike had a broken leg bone

but he would be all right.

Sally was badly hurt.

She lay very still.

The doctors wanted to contact

her mum and dad

but they didn't know who she was

or where she lived.

Mike had been given an injection

to make him sleep

and so he couldn't tell them.

They asked the police to help.

At home, Sally's dad sat still.

He'd been so cross with Sally

that at first he hadn't thought

she might have been hurt.

Now he was afraid.

The doorbell rang.

Sally's dad rushed to open the door.

Outside, there was a policeman.

He said there had been an accident

and he would take them

to see Sally in hospital.

Only her dad could go.

Her mother had to find someone

to look after the other children.

At the hospital,

a nurse took him to see Sally

who was badly hurt.

When he saw Sally,

her dad wanted to cry.

She looked so young and so ill.

'That's my girl!' he said in horror.

The doctors operated on Sally

for much of the night.

When she was taken to the ward,

her mum and dad sat by her bed.

Sally's mum cried and cried

until, in the end, she fell asleep.

Sally lay very still in the bed.

Nurses came in and out

to see how she was.

The sun began to rise.

The birds began to sing.

Sally's dad stood up.

As he did so, Sally opened her eyes.

She was very drowsy

and didn't know where she was.

Her dad took her hand.

'You'll be all right, Sal,'

he told her softly.

A nurse came in.

She was pleased to see Sally awake.

'You seem to have had a fight

with a motorbike,' she said.

Sally's mum woke up.

When she saw that Sally was awake,

she began to cry again.

Sally's legs were so badly hurt

that she couldn't walk.

She was told she would have to use

a wheel chair for some time.

Sally couldn't bear it –

she cried and cried.

Mike went to see her every day.

At first, Sally's mum and dad

were very angry with him.

They said he was to blame.

But, after a time,

they knew how sorry he was

and how much

he was helping Sally

to start life again.

CPSIA information can be obtained
at www.ICGtesting.com
Printed in the USA
LVOW10s1627210217
524951LV00002B/394/P